A simple Formula that EVERYBODY can use to irresistibly capture and instantly guide ANYONE'S attention towards more choices and freedom.

What parents are saying about the book...

If you have a teenager in your family, you owe this book to yourself. Full of practical advice, powerful techniques, and real-life examples that can help you connect with your teen as it did for me with my 17-year-old son.

-Jennet Appova
UN Officer, New York, New York

I resorted to this book when I became desperate about our interaction with my teenage son. For a few years, we had little, if any communication, and even when we did, it consisted of me explaining to him what to do and how, what is good and bad for him, and him impatiently interrupting me with an "ok, ok, ok." While I realized that this was not working, I was clueless about what to do.

With this book's help, I repaired our broken communication and now achieve so much more. For the first time in quite a long time, I had an over hour-long interesting and sincere conversation with my son. I felt that he was not only listening to me, but he was also really engaged in the conversation we were having. I was the first one to say goodbye (!) and he called me in a week (!), himself, to share some news and happenings in his college life. For the first time in such a long time, HE called me. I am so happy!

The book is well written and offers easy-to-follow guidelines. It gave me so many "aha" moments that I had to stop and think; the power of a question was the real eye opener for me and once I started using it, I became more convinced of its hidden potential as an important step in problem solving. I like that the author came up with her ideas when she started asking herself questions about how to best deal with her teen.

The beauty of this book's approach is its astonishing simplicity and the ease of applying the suggestions. You can start using it almost immediately after reading, as I did, and, over time, you will become better at doing it. In one conversation with my son, I used all the suggested tricks and saw immediate results.

I should also stress that the book is more universal than it claims. You can absolutely use these methods to communicate with anyone, not just your child, and you do not have to have communication problems to benefit from it. There is always room to improve what you already have. I started with my son and I went on to use it with my students, friends, family, colleagues, and just about everyone, including myself.

-Gayane Hovakimian
Professor, New York, New York

I have read your wonderful book! It is outstanding! I remember and usually use the techniques, but sometimes I slip back into bad communication, so I recommend re-reading the book from time to time. And the illustrations are PERFECT! They communicate your ideas so well! I would like to be one of the first to purchase a bunch of copies to have one on every floor of the house and enough to share with friends.

The approach is great for teens but it is also about ME! When I adopted this affirmative way of communicating with my children and with all people, I too felt so much better about life… I am in a dramatically better mood when I talk about kids being on time in the morning, instead of being in a bad mood because I am talking about kids being late. Because I'm visualizing it too – and I am so much happier when I am visualizing my kids doing the right thing. And since you opened my eyes to this, I have found that throughout all areas of life in business, and socially, and in the family, talking constructively to people gets better results 100% of the time. If I say "Dad doesn't want Chinese food," someone else says "Well I do!" But, if I say "Dad would love to try something different for dinner tonight, any ideas?" Then someone says "yes, let's try …." Everybody is happy and so am I because I have completely avoided spreading negativity. Your book is AMAZING and everyone should read it!

Your coaching formulas are so much more than a simple improvement of something – they are a liberating thing, a whole permanent life change! They help you to live life better and enjoy life more and from that come all the other little improvements.

-Allison Moore
Artist, Westchester, New York

Your book and language are amazing. I think you have found that simple and affordable way to help in a practical means. Though my teen lives in the UK, I use your formula with him all the time whenever we communicate! At the same time, the topics and examples you've given in the book reach far beyond the teenage years.

I strongly believe that this is just the first of many books for you. I can't wait to see an entire series about different aspects of this wonderful life and funny beings that we can sometimes meet throughout the journey! Tomorrow I am flying for a business trip and I can't wait to try out "Please don't take me to the airport." on the taxi driver. I just want to use the technique to see what happens."

-Aram Akopyan, MD, Ph.D.
Sidney, Australia

Viktoria's strategies for helping me guide my son to make good decisions have been invaluable. Instead of arguing, we now envision good outcomes that work for both of us. This has tremendously shifted my ability to help him achieve his goals.

-Julie Scott
Nutritionist, Attorney, Palo Alto, California

This is a great, concise, book. I wish that I would have

had it when I was muddling through with my own teenagers; I recognized so many of the feelings and situations Viktoria writes about, especially - and worst of all — a huge sense of failed parenting. Reading Viktoria's book, I can see, happily, that parenting is never over and the skills she presents are useful no matter what stage we find ourselves in. She focuses on the real skills of communication (vividly illustrated by universal situations), making it easy to adapt them to one's own circumstances. The book's brevity makes it a very excellent guide. Perhaps one day, it will be a chapter in a longer work - still easy to use - because Viktoria's coaching and systems are so brilliant.

-Pru, Massachusetts

This book is another solid piece of advice I was very fortunate to receive from Viktoria. The formula is the perfect practical tool. It's a combination of art and science that you can use immediately to change how we speak to our teens and ourselves. Schools and peers don't always teach us the most important things; either life teaches you the hard way or you are lucky enough to learn them in the family. I want to be that family for my only child and this practical science-based framework is now the tool we use to speak to our teens and ourselves.

-JV, Lawyer
Mother, New York, New York

The high quality of Viktoria's book and Formula are not a surprise to me because I have known her for several years and even took her training sessions. My children are grown up and I am sorry that I didn't know all these possibilities when I was raising my teens and they were causing me challenges. Fortunately, the book and Viktoria's approaches aren't only for parents; they are life tips and smart tricks that touch upon the key points in any relationship. With this knowledge, I personally developed new effective skills in my everyday communication with my children, colleagues, patients, and students. I hope that if life enables me to be involved in the upbringing of my grandchildren, then, first I will strongly recommend this approach and the book to my kids, and second I will "correct my errors" when spending time with my own grandkids.

-Armine Hakobyan, M.D.
Assistant Professor, Yerevan, Armenia

The book is tremendous! With very little effort I am now able to have great influence in my communication. I successfully use the concepts of Viktoria's book with people of all ages, be that a five-year-old child, teens or independent well-developed adults. It always works! I enjoyed the clarity and preciseness of the explanations in the book. The illustrations are useful, fun and expressive. I can recommend it to anyone - be sure, it will both improve your interaction quality with people around you and reduce the stress of problems with miscommunication.

-Narine Karamyan
Mother, Writer, Poet, Artist, Cairo, Egypt

Not only do I use Viktoria's AGQ concepts when I brainstorm in certain sticky situations with my 12-year-old daughter, but I also use them for myself too. Instead of going into the problem loop, I ask myself "do you have control over what is going on?" or "can you change what is happening?" If the answer to one or both is no, it is easier to look at alternative solutions. So, instead of saying to myself that I have a problem, now I say, "Ok, what can I do to solve this?" The concept is so easy to understand and use. This approach has saved me several times from down-spiraling into deeper anxiety and more stress!

-Archanaa Shyam
Dublin, California

One of the best pieces of advice about parenting that I have ever received.

-Cathy, Mother of two teens
Scarsdale, New York

"Want Your Teen to Listen?" gives straight-forward techniques that work! I am really paying close attention to the words I use with my 15-year old now. I focus my and his attention to what I would like for him to do rather than what I don't want. Just this morning when my son wanted to sleep in, I said "Sleeping in feels good but this is a choice for being late to school. It's your choice. Do you want to be on-time or late to school?" Then he jumped up and got ready! I have used a parenting system, "Positive Discipline for Teens," but using the formula from "Want Your Teen to Listen?" has been a great enhancement, making the parenting system I use much more effective and efficient.

-Louann Tung, Ph.D.
Parenting Coach, Livermore, California

NOTE: The author is grateful to those who have provided testimonials and fully respects those clients who wanted to contribute, but for privacy reasons did not want their names or titles to be used.

WANT YOUR TEEN TO LISTEN?

The Proven Irresistible Formula
to Get Your Teen
to Cooperate and Avoid the
Wrong Crowd and Bad Choices

Viktoria Ter-Nikoghosyan, Ph.D.

San Francisco, 2017

WANT YOUR TEEN TO LISTEN?
The Proven Irresistible Formula
to Get Your Teen to Cooperate
and Avoid the Wrong Crowd and Bad Choices

Copyright © 2017 by Viktoria Ter-Nikoghosyan

www.Live-in-Harmony.com

All rights reserved. No part of this publication may be reproduced, distributed, or transmitted in any form or by any means, including photocopying, recording, or other electronic or mechanical methods, without the prior written permission of the publisher, except in the case of brief quotations embodied in critical reviews and certain other non-commercial uses permitted by copyright law.

For permission requests, write to tervika@Live-in-Harmony.com

Development and Final Copy Editing by Janice Forry
JForry34@gmail.com
Copy Editing by Bettyanne Green
Front Cover Illustration by Mihran Akopyan
Front Cover Design by Janice Forry
Book Illustrations by Viktoria Ter-Nikoghosyan

ISBN 9781543162400

HOW ARE YOU DOING AS A PARENT?
Take a free self-assessment to help you find out at
www.Live-in-Harmony.com/parenting-teens

CONTENTS

Acknowledgements
Preface
Chapter 1
Are You Losing Connection with Your Teen?   1
Chapter 2
How To Capture and Keep Your Teen's Attention   13
Chapter 3
How To Get Your Teen to Listen and Follow   27
Chapter 4
How To Keep Your Teen Listening With Negation   47
Chapter 5
How To Get Irresistible Instant Cooperation With Your Teen   63
Conclusion
How to Recall the AGQ^{SM} Formula Every Time You Speak   81
About the Author   93

DEDICATION

I am indebted to Dr. Richard Bandler, whose genius in finding simple, fast-working and easy solutions for humans to excel has inspired me to find a simple parenting formula. Thank you!

To my husband, three children and two granddaughters - thank you for coming and staying in my world to share fun and laughter!

ACKNOWLEDGEMENTS

Above all, I would like to thank my family for their trust and patience. My husband, David, has always been stalwart in showing support during my pioneer efforts in all the fields in which I have worked.

My teenage daughter, Maneh, deserves special thanks, not only for being my greatest motivation to find a formula, but also for being my best guinea pig in our home "laboratory" and my best assistant, helping me film during workshops and then transcribing it all.

Thanks to my youngest son's, Meesh's persistence to understand, I have added more examples, revised sections of the book, and learned to transform my terrible drawn stick figures into computer friendly stick figures. I also need to thank my oldest son for reminding me to be concise by recommending shortening the book as much as possible to make it easy learning. The comments and suggestions from my youngest daughter-in-law, Valentina, were invaluable.

Friends and clients (some of whom have been both) have also helped me to no end; not only were these parents, teachers, and professors sources of inspiration for the book, but they were also generous in reading and giving feedback on the manuscript and on how the formula works. Teens, especially and thankfully, mirrored parental behavior, giving me their observations about how their parents talk and a lot of feedback on my approach.

The book and my relationship with teens, whether it be my own daughter or those of clients, would have suffered greatly if not for the work of scientists who discovered what asking questions does to our brains. For enabling me to know why questions are so powerful I would like to thank: Dr. Colin P. Doherty, W. Caroline West, Ph.D., Laura C. Dilley, Ph.D., Dr. Stefanie Shattuck-Hufnagel, and David Caplan, M.D., Ph.D.

Without the support of designers and editors, the book would probably still be in the works. Janice Forry, a brilliant content and copy editor and dear friend, was my biggest critic as a mother of three teenagers. Even with all of her "but Viktoria..." comments, she was unique in nurturing my creative process and bringing out the best in my work. She not only made my writing and our teamwork fun and enjoyable, but she also encouraged me to start two more books and gave practical design advice on publishing.

I am also thankful to copy editor, Bettyanne Green, for getting so easily adjusted to my fast discussion style, asking the right questions and sharing a fun work style.

I would also like to acknowledge and thank Bernard Langan whose insightful and sharp editing made some parts of the text sparkle with clarity and more congruent with my own methods.

And last, but not least, I was blessed to learn from Dr. Richard Bandler how to feel good and be happy for absolutely no reason. Your genius work and teaching have brought lasting and dramatic changes not only to my life but also to my family, friends, and clients. I am deeply grateful!

PREFACE

I help parents who go through traumatic daily stress because of various issues with their teens. All the parents with whom I have worked were well-intentioned and well-educated, with many parenting workshops and books under their belts. Yet with all this knowledge, these parents were still struggling with and overwhelmed by their teens. They battled daily with feelings of incompetence as they faced eye rolls, heated or suppressed conflicts with their teens, or worse - blank stares and complete apathy. All parents were exhausted from the stress and searching for a solution.

Does this sound like you? Have you ever had the feeling that your teen doesn't listen to you or even register that you are speaking to him or her? Does your teen talk back or have a disrespectful attitude? Do you feel like your family values have been overridden? Are you afraid that your teen will choose the wrong crowd and get into trouble with the law? Are you having sleepless nights because of your teen's behavior? Is your teen's behavior making you face extra bills for legal or medical fees?

This describes how I was when my daughter hit her thirteenth birthday – feeling helpless. Despite all the success I had had in coaching and consulting, I frequently could not "connect" with my own daughter. She was gradually drifting away and seemed constantly preoccupied with her crowd of friends, whether in person or virtually. As with many parents, I feared she would choose the wrong path or fall prey to peer pressure. I felt frustrated and wondered what I was doing wrong and which skills I was lacking.

Figure 1: Teens constantly surrounded virtually by their friends

Like many parents, I wanted a universal formula, a shortcut, a magic spell of sorts, **to help me protect,**

guide and assist my teen in any given situation no matter my teen's or my mood.

So, I took parenting courses and workshops, but I couldn't find anything to help me *always* get my daughter's attention and cooperation in an easy way. I decided to do my own research and studied everything from the workings of the teenage brain to behavioral patterns and linguistics to parenting and how to grab someone's attention. My background in science helped me delve into scientific journals, extrapolate and interpret the results I found there, and combine these with my experience from coaching and consulting.

I didn't find any formulas in my investigation, but I did find fascinating and not commonly known pieces of information on how the human mind works. After a year of intensive interdisciplinary research, I put all these pieces together and **developed the effective and easily applicable system that I present in this book**. It works wonders in any situation. **The system solved the issues** with my daughter and has helped many of my clients in my coaching practice.

What has parents at their wits' end?

I whittled down the long list of parental complaints, and came up with three main problematic areas for parents:

- Teens do not listen and cooperate
- Teens sometimes bring out the worst in you

because they frustrate you so much

- Teens fight with you every time they hear the word "no"

Effective solutions for helping your teen to listen and cooperate can be found in one simple formula or shortcut, based on the science and art of cooperation. Once you master this formula, you will be confident in guiding and guarding your teen in any situation, and securing your family's peacefulness for now and the future.

This book presents the formula that helped me to get out of those two years of struggle and uncertainty with my teen. It helped me build a path back to my daughter in just a couple of weeks. The skills in this formula now enable me to maintain my daughter's trust so that she feels comfortable coming to me when she needs guidance or advice. Of course, we still have minor disagreements, and she isn't always happy with my decisions, but she knows that I have her best interests in mind. We spend more quality and happy time together. She even brings her friends home to ask me for help. Her friends tell her, "Your mom listens." What they don't realize is that not only do I listen, but I also apply the formulas that I have developed!

Each chapter of this book builds upon the other, starting with identifying common communication issues and concluding with how to solve them. This sequence is designed to help you to learn my formula gradually and to integrate it as you read, which will help you recall it when you need it.

You'll learn how to capture your teen's undivided attention and motivate him or her to cooperate. You will be able to help your teens make better choices in their teen years and to become independent, well-balanced and happy adults.

The formula in this book helped many of my clients to manage with ease, success, and elegance those curve balls that frequently derail and traumatize us in the "dreaded" teen years. My clients' feedback on the formula is very positive; they have had huge success in establishing mutually respectful relationships with their teens.

Parents love that this formula is revolutionary in its simplicity, that it has instantaneous impact and provides lasting results.

My wish for you is that this book will help you, as it has so many others, to reconnect with your teen and bring laughter and joy back into your lives.

CHAPTER 1

Are You Losing Connection with Your Teen?

> *"I define connection as the energy that exists between people when they feel seen, heard, and valued; when they can give and receive without judgment; and when they derive sustenance and strength from the relationship."*
>
> *— Brené Brown*

Over the past few years, the most frequent complaint that I have heard from parents is that their kids do not listen. I find that what this typically means is that the kids do not do what the parents want or advise them to do. This resistance is often followed by disrespectful behavior such as talking back, whining or nagging. With great frustration, parents express that their teens don't take responsibility for their actions, and instead argue about everything.

Often parents feel helpless when facing a conflict with their teens. At home, parents may venture into solving the problem, but in public most avoid conflicts altogether. Do you ever find yourself feeling out of control and hearing the 'ugly' you shouting at your teen, "What's wrong with you?" and, "You don't try hard enough!" Or even, "I can't wait until you are old enough to move out!" Instances that could be used to teach or model behavior for a teen can feel like energy-consuming power struggles that sometimes push parents to the edge.

Have you ever heard yourself complaining about how difficult it is to parent teens? Have you been saying things to your teens that you thought you would never say? Do you feel like you have completely lost connection with that young person living in your home? Have you ever felt helpless as a parent or exasperated when communicating with your teen?

For many parents, putting into practice what they have learned from parenting books or workshops feels impossible. Somehow success in communicating with their teens has been elusive, and getting a teen's cooperation even more so. Some parents, especially those who always feel busy with work, also complain that even the most popular parenting systems are too complicated and time-consuming to remember and apply.

What does communication really mean?

Let's take a look at communication for a bit.

We communicate to get an outcome. An effective communicator, however, is not just someone with a good command of language and delivery. According to Gregory Bateson, the meaning of communication is the response you get. He further explains: *"From what I say, it may be possible to make predictions about how you will answer. My words contain meaning or information about your reply."*[1]

A good communicator registers and adjusts accordingly to the verbal and non-verbal response of the receiver. So, I would define communication as "a two-way information sharing process that involves one party sending a message that is received, processed and responded to by the receiving party, in a way that the expressing party realizes that the message was received."

---

[1] Gregory Bateson, *Steps to an Ecology of Mind: Collected Essays in Anthropology Psychiatry*, University of Chicago Press, 1972.
[2] Sara Kehaulani Goo, 'The Skills Americans Say Kids Need to Succeed in

According to a 2015 Pew Research Center[2] survey, 90% of American adults said that the ability to communicate well was the most important skill for their children to learn in order to get ahead in society today. This is a huge shift in values from the emphasis on math, reading, and science. We know communication is important and we want our kids to do it well, yet simple surveys show that people's main complaint is that the other party (our child, spouse, anybody) does not receive the information. "They don't listen!" or "They do not hear me!" Communication is blocked.

Was it always that way? Or is this only a new, recent phenomenon? We do not need research to notice the obvious: We (our kids even more) are constantly bombarded by visual and auditory information from TVs, phones, computers, tablets, texts and social media. This flood entertains, and keeps us virtually and visually crowded and busy, pulling our attention in several directions, as if we're constantly dealing with many people simultaneously. This is one reason that we lose important connection with our teens. **We now need to put extra effort into capturing the other person's attention, especially if the other person, someone like your teen, is obviously more impacted by this flood of information.**

---

[2] Sara Kehaulani Goo, 'The Skills Americans Say Kids Need to Succeed in Life', *FACTTANK: News in the Numbers*, Pew Research Center, 19 February 2015 (http://www.pewresearch.org/fact-tank/2015/02/19/skills-for-success/).

Figure 2: Teens drowning in information

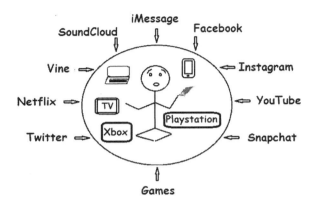

I raised two successful sons (37 and 30 years old) who'd gone through their teen years without social media. When my daughter came along several years later, I thought I would be well prepared for her teen years. I was doing well until she hit thirteen. Suddenly, it was as if she stopped hearing what I was saying. She often seemed distracted and removed. As soon as I noticed this, I did my best to reconnect, and I thought my skills and experience as a personal coach and mom were enough. Alas, I could not connect with her in the way I wanted, and I felt as if I had been hit by a curve ball.

One incident proved particularly painful. While my whole family was on vacation and our house was empty, my daughter's new friends, three 15-year-olds from good families broke into our house to party with their friends for the entire week we were gone. Luckily, they didn't trash our house, but they did all the things teens do when they party. After getting the police involved, I sat questioning where I had gone wrong, wondering where I had failed in teaching my daughter to choose friends. I was surprised because those girls had been in my home several times, even for sleepovers!

After talking to the girls' parents, I realized that they were loving and caring, but also lost, struggling with how to deal with their teens. I also felt lost, but for different reasons: I couldn't sleep at night fearing that because of my inability to communicate with my daughter successfully, she could become a disconnected teen who would easily succumb to peer pressure. Had social media taken over the role of parent? As a coach, I teach communication skills, but where had I failed in communicating what would protect and guide her to make better choices?

When did we stop being our child's Trusted Advisor?

Through analyzing the problem, I found that these days, children and teens are flooded with information, not only from peers in person but even more prevalently so from the virtual world. Teens, in general, are less available to communicate with their parents. According to a *Psychology Today* article, one study found that kids were so immersed in technology that they greeted their parents on arrival home from work only 30% of the time and completely ignored them 50% of the time.[3] A 2016 report from Common Sense Media, Inc., a non-profit organization, found that of 1200 parents and teens surveyed, 66% of parents think their teens spend too much time on their mobile devices and 52% of teens agree. Of the teens surveyed, 78% admitted that they check their devices at least once hourly.[4]

As most parents have expressed to me, digital technology is everywhere and their teens often know how to use it better than their parents do. Plus, as teens grow up they want more independence, all of which makes it difficult for parents to remain their Trusted Advisor.

As I mentioned, when my daughter was 13-15 years old I wasn't always able to get her full attention. Sometimes I could reach her and she would take in my guidance or help, but most of the time I could not. Often, she would nod her head confirming that she had heard and understood my request. Then I would double-check to ensure she intended to do whatever I had asked, for example, locking the gate.

> "Honey, would you please lock the gate? That cat got in again and dug up my flowers."

> "Hmm..."

---

[3] Jim Taylor, Ph.D., 'Is Technology Creating a Family Divide', *Psychology Today*, 13 March 2013.
[4] Common Sense Media, *Technology Addiction: Concern, Controversy, and Finding Balance*, May 2016.

"Honey, did you hear me? I asked you to lock the gate."

"Yes, I heard you. I will."

I believed her. Then she did not do it. In a bit, she would say that we had not talked about that topic or I had never asked.

This was so frustrating! None of my skills were working effectively!

How this book is different

Most of the parenting books and classes I found taught parents how to be an active, effective or responsive listener, and how to love your kids, praise them or discipline them using a system. Actually, about 90% of what parents are taught emphasizes listening skills because, I believe, it is easier to describe, structure and teach parents elements of listening than those of expressing. So far, I have found nothing on how to communicate with teens to get their attention, or how to share your knowledge and experience with them directly in an easy and fast way. This book is a crucial step in proactive communication needed to improve parent-teen relationships.

What are we parents doing wrong?

In my research and analyses, I discovered that there are generally three mistakes that parents make with their teens:

1) Fail to grab the teen's full attention first

2) Steer their teen in the wrong or no direction

3) Fail to motivate the teen and get their cooperation

Think about this for a minute. Do you always have your teen's attention when you are trying to communicate something? Do they follow your advice or guidance? Can you always motivate them to behave in ways that will help and not harm them in the long run? Do you always understand them? Can you get into a calm and controlled state to communicate with your teen in the way you want?

There is a way!

There is a simple way to communicate with your teen as I learned to do. Precisely, this means capturing their full attention and conveying your guidance in a way that adds choices. This leads them to cooperate, make better choices and avoid or stop behavior that is not useful. There is a way!

Out of love and necessity I drew upon all my unique knowledge, skills and resources to create a **concise formula and system**. I can now easily guide and guard my daughter by getting her undivided attention and cooperation; I know what to say and how to say it respectfully and effectively. Moreover, I can catch her attention instantly and offer her choices so that my guidance has a quality that she cannot help but consider. And, so importantly, this system enables her to trust that she can come to me whenever she needs guidance and advice.

My formula and system can help you do all this adeptly and conversationally!!!

Remember, effective and adept communication is a two-way exchange. In this time of information overload when our teens' brains are constantly engaged, we need to put extra effort into learning new skills to converse with teens to get the responses and outcomes that we want. The communication skills I have developed have been so valuable in my life when I needed to act quickly, effectively and almost effortlessly.

Learning and demonstrating effective listening and expressing skills is **how we can inspire our children and give them opportunities to model us, motivate them to improve their communication skills and empower them to get ahead in their life confidently.**

I invite you to find out how to finally bring peace and fun back into your family. Continue reading and you will learn the skills that have helped thousands of other well-meaning, well-educated parents assist their teens in growing up healthy, happy and ready to launch into the world.

CHAPTER 2

How to Capture and Keep Your Teen's Attention

> *"A good teacher, like a good entertainer, first must hold his audience's attention, then he can teach his lesson."*
>
> *— John Henrik Clarke*

"It's as if my words go in one ear and out the other." How many times can you recall thinking this after failing to capture your teen's attention? Maybe you have the feeling that your words just bounce back like you have been talking to a wall. And even if they nod, you can see that they weren't really listening.

This was how I felt.

The realization came on one of those days when my daughter called me perhaps six times crying:

"Mom, I am sorry. I forgot the key again. I am so sorry. Please come and open the door. I will never forget it again. I promise."

This happened when we were living in New York. It was a cold winter day and she could not go to any neighbors because we had just moved there. So, I canceled my meeting and drove back to the house. I kept thinking, "I constantly remind her and she definitely understands and wants to remember, but something is not working." That was the moment when I realized that I was doing something wrong.

I sat in the car in the parking lot with my hands on my head and wondered: Is there one simple communication tool that could dramatically improve how I get and hold her attention? If I am doing something wrong, then what is right? Is there a way to find out and always know what to say so that she would remember? I wanted to be more influential! I wanted my words to have instant impact! Yes, I was dreaming!

This inspired my quest to find a communication tool to help my situation, but I didn't discover the answer from one particular source. What I did find was a lot of useful information that when put together became the very tool for which I had searched. I tried this tool with my children, clients, shared it with friends, family members, and colleagues. This was the formula or shortcut about which I had dreamt and it works!

The formula consists of three steps. The first is to capture your teens' attention in a way that they cannot help but listen.

How can we reach this first step in any communication, meaning how to capture a person's attention to begin the process of getting the response we want, in other words, to influence? Here are the main highlights from my findings that have helped me. You can understand and use them right away!

There are several different ways to ask someone a question. The most obvious way is a direct address.

#1: Asking Questions Directly

I researched teaching, marketing, politics, science, engineering, parenting and coaching to find out which influencing tools are the most common, used most frequently, and the most effective. All these fields, in one way or another, emphasize that **asking questions is the main tool to get desired response in your communication**.

We communicate mostly by making statements, sometimes by asking questions and, not as rarely as we think, by giving commands (imperatives).

Think about what types of sentences you use with your teens when you instruct, guide, advise or simply tell them what to do or not to do. Do any of these sound familiar?

> Wake up!
> Do your homework!
> No partying!
> No smoking!
> Clean your room!
> Put your laundry in the basket!

Yes, I have exaggerated, but only a bit! I invite you to pay attention to your conversations, you might be surprised!

We ask questions to gather information, understand, learn, satisfy our curiosity, test other people's knowledge (exams, interviews), make a point (rhetorical questions), and have a guide for research (Socratic method). The additional benefits of questioning can be to show respect, gain trust, and build relationships.

As a coach, I learned that asking effective questions is an important skill to master. There are many powerful questions that I observed have tremendous impact and I wanted to know *why* they were so effective.

Why, as Joseph Jordania finds[5], does asking questions distinguish us from animals and, more interestingly for my quest, influence us so profoundly? Does it affect us on a behavioral level, or on a deeper more physiological or molecular level? I started exploring questions and their impact from different perspectives. I wanted to find a scientific explanation and behavioral confirmation. I spent almost two years researching and questioning many people. I found that scientists already had some answers and the only thing I needed to do was to combine these answers together!

I finally found a study that answered my main query about questions: a 2004 fMRI study of the brain[6] revealed that the human brain responds differently to questions than to statements. Certain areas of the brain get activated when questions are asked with a rising intonation at the end of the sentence (indicated by the arrow in Figure 3) in comparison to statements and questions with falling intonation.

---

[5] Joseph Jordania, 'Who Asked the First Question? The Origins of Human Choral Singing, Intelligence, Language and Speech', Programme "Logos", Tbilisi, Georgia, 2006.

[6] Colin P. Doherty, W. Caroline West, Laura C. Dilley, Stefanie Shattuck-Hufnagel, and David Caplan, 'Question/Statement Judgments: An fMRI Study of Intonation Processing', *Human Brain Mapping*, Volume 23, Issue 2, pages 85–98, October 2004.

Figure 3: The power of intonation

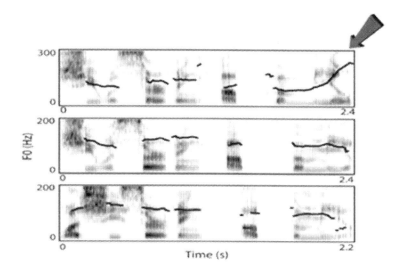

Three paired stimuli illustrating the different intonation conditions in the experiment. The data set consists of voice spectrographs with uncorrected fundamental frequency (pitch) contours super- imposed as a dark black line. From top to bottom: an RQ (Rising Question) utterance (*She was serving up the meal?*), an FS (Falling Statement) utterance (*She was serving up the meal*), and an FQ (Falling Question) utterance (*Was she serving up the meal*). (Figure created using PRAAT software.)

#2 Asking Questions Nonverbally

Excited with what I found, I searched further. Since 80-93%[7] of our communication is non-verbal, then my obvious next question was: "Does the brain similarly discriminate non-verbal and written questions and statements?"

Based on observation, infants can ask questions even before using words by just making some sounds with a rising intonation at the end. Later, toddlers use single words and then phrases with rising intonation at the end, such as "Mommy?" for what might be, "Where is Mommy?" Do these examples bring back memories of your own teen as a toddler?

Even though non-verbal clues, such as a raised eyebrow or tilt of the head, play a large role in communicating questions, raising the intonation at the end of a sentence has more leverage in triggering brain activation simply because you can capture a person's attention when they look away and do not see your non-verbal clue.

---

[7] Albert Mehrabian, 'Silent Messages: Implicit Communication of Emotions and Attitudes', Wadsworth Publishing Company, July 1972.

#3 Our minds cannot NOT answer questions

Our minds can make sense of most any piece of information that comes to its attention. Asking questions is like waving a flag at the start line, where the brain cannot help but look for an answer. Hence, the double negation – the brain cannot NOT answer questions. The brain relentlessly searches for a meaning to understand the information, and for that, it goes inside accumulated internal experience and finds some similarities to which it can relate. This process is called Transderivational Search (TDS), "a psychological and cybernetics term for when a search is being conducted for a fuzzy match across a broad field."[8]

Now let's put all this together

When we ask a question, we activate certain processes in the brain and the mind goes into that relentless search to find meaning and come up with an answer. **It happens instantaneously!** We may not necessarily get a verbal or nonverbal answer that we can hear or see, but the brain will eventually find some answer to make sense of the question asked. Many influential leaders use this phenomenon, knowing perhaps intuitively, how to activate minds and create the pictures they want in our minds. I call it "we cannot NOT answer questions." It reminds me of Axiom #1, "one

---

[8] Jaap Boonstra and Leon de Caluwe, *Intervening and Changing: Looking for Meaning in Interactions*, John Wiley & Sons, 2007.

cannot NOT communicate" of Paul Watzlawick's Five Axioms about communication[9].

So, by asking questions, we *make* people hear us because we activate their brains and send them searching for an answer. In other words, **we make them listen**. Remember, hearing is when a noise or vibration is carried from our ear to the brain; it's an involuntary process. Listening is an act of choice: it's when our brains decide to make sense of that noise or vibration. Questions induce listening in a way that triggers the brain, sending it searching to find an answer. If asked correctly, questions can bring about a behavioral change.

Would you like to try it out?

Go ahead and test this knowledge for yourself: Pay close attention to how people react when you deliberately ask a direct question and with a rising intonation at the end of it. They will pause for a split second when the question (and perhaps the answer) is familiar—the pause may be so brief you might not even notice. If the question is unfamiliar, you will get a longer pause.

You can use this tool with anyone: your boss, children, spouse, co-workers, etc. You can even try it out with infants: When you ask with raised intonation at the end

---

[9] Paul Watzlawick and John H. Weakland, ed. *The Interactional View: studies at the Mental Research Institute, Palo Alto, 1965-1974*, 1977.

of a question, they will pause. (Make sure to ask loudly because infants can only distinguish loud sounds!) If used correctly, it can have a huge impact! And even when people know that you are using this technique, it'll still work because the brain finds it irresistible to attempt to answer questions. It's an automatic response, like jumping when we hear a sudden loud noise. It is unnatural *not* to react to it.

Figuring out the 'why' behind what makes asking questions such an influential tool was my big 'AHA' moment. That 'why' made me ask questions deliberately whenever I wanted to catch and hold anybody's attention.

So, that's it: the irresistible instant-impact skill to catch and hold anyone's attention!

If you want to catch and hold your teen's attention, ask a question instead of stating something, threatening or giving a command!

Figure 4 (A-C): Parent asking questions versus making statements and giving commands

A)

B)

c)

Moreover, using this skill is going to have a ripple effect. As with any transformative knowledge and skill, as soon as you apply it (not even needing to master it) your family members will learn it, apply it and benefit in the same transformative way.

> ### A CLIENT'S SUCCESS STORY
>
> *After I described how frustrated I felt that my teenagers didn't seem to pay attention to what I told or asked them to do, Viktoria wisely advised me to "ask them questions instead of telling them what to do." I've since become more conscious about how I communicate with my kids and have been pleasantly surprised to find that when I ask a question of them, they stop what they're doing and engage in conversation with me. That is one of the best pieces of advice about parenting that I have ever received.*

It's important to exercise caution: Asking questions is a powerful tool, so you need to be **careful what kind of question you ask,** because it is possible to unintentionally harm someone in the process.

The next chapter gives you an idea of what type of question to ask in any situation to get your desired response. Remember as William Blake said, "If there is a question – there must be an answer."

CHAPTER 3

How to Get Your Teen to Listen and Follow

> "You get what you focus on,
> so focus on what you want."
>
> — *Anonymous*

Can you shift your teen's focus of attention and add choices? The answer is - Yes, you can!

By switching to asking questions instead of making statements, I got my daughter's attention any time I wanted, but for some reason, I still didn't always get the results I wanted. Why? Again, another why! Was this just because of her being a teen? Was she going against my advice just to find her own identity? Or, was there something else? Why could I always get other people to consider what I was saying, but not her?

So, I was on my journey of searching for a formula for **how to ask the right questions**.

People perceive, process, store, communicate and learn information through the five senses: hearing, sight, touch, taste, and smell. For most people, three senses (visual, auditory and kinesthetic) dominate our perceptions. Of course, we need them all, but we tend to use a mixture of them when we process impulses and information, developing our own learning styles. Different studies have concluded that 50-65% of the adult population prefer the visual modality for learning, 30-35% auditory and 5-15% kinesthetic.[10]

Do you know the power of the visual sense?

So yes, we perceive the world around us only through our senses. There are no other means. And one sense dominates considerably! More than 50% of our brain is devoted to processing visual information.[11] Why is this? Around 90-95% of information that we receive comes

---

[10] For instance, see Walter Burke Barbe, Raymond H. Swassing, Michael N. Milone, Jr. (June 1979). *Teaching Through Modality Strengths: Concepts and Practices*. Columbus, Ohio: Zaner-Blosner. and Gloria M. Thompson, *Bridging the Gap: Moving Toward a Blended Learning Environment*, MMA Fall Educators' Conference – 2003 (http://www.mmaglobal.org/publications/Proceedings/2003-MMA-Fall-Educators-Conference-Proceedings.pdf#page=136)
or University of Alabama School of Medicine
(http://www.uab.edu/uasomume/fd2/visuals/page1.htm)

[11] Susan Hagen, *The Mind's Eye: How do we transform an ever-changing jumble of visual stimuli into the rich and coherent three-dimensional perception we know as sight? Rochester vision scientists are helping reshape our understanding of how the brain 'sees.'* University of Rochester
(http://www.rochester.edu/pr/Review/V74N4/0402_brainscience.htl)

through visual images that are taken in and processed quickly, in comparison to hearing, tactile or sensation.[12] Visual perception in learning is used the most because it is most efficient.[13]

> "You sound so stupid; can't you see it?" This caught my attention while watching a TV show, Judge Judy to be precise. We do not see sounds, right? The expression "I see" predominantly means, "I understand."

We understand better when we see, because sight is the fastest channel to simultaneously take in most non-linear information. When we listen, we receive linear information, which is not processed as fast as visual impulses. Moreover, optic nerves are 40 times faster and pass on 25 times more information than auditory nerves.[14] In one of my native languages, Russian, there is a proverb: "It is better to see something once than to hear it 100 times." The English version of this: **"A picture is worth a thousand words."**

---

[12] John C. Russ, *The Image Processing Handbook*, Fifth Edition, CRC Press, Dec 19, 2006, p.83.

[13] Michael I. Posner, Mary J Nissen, Raymond M. Klein, Visual dominance: An information-processing account of its origins and significance. *Psychological Review*, Vol 83(2), March 1976, p. 157-171. (http://dx.doi.org/10.1037/0033-295X.83.2.157)

[14] Based on the studies of neuroscientists such as Robert Ornstein, Leslie Hart, Bert Decker and Joseph Ledoux. - Patrick M. Georges, Anne-Sophie Bayle Tourtoulou, Michel Badoc, *Neuromarketing in Action: How to Talk and Sell to the Brain*, Kogan Page, 2013.

What does our brain do with these visual images?

Most people do not realize that **images (still or moving) are attached to the words** they think. Some people argue that what we say is just words, but words cannot exist by themselves! They have to be attached to and carried by one of our senses. There is no other way for thoughts with words to happen. Every word is connected to an image and/or a sound or inner voice! Visual images can be internal or external images.

The most fascinating discovery for me in my coaching career was to learn, and then experience firsthand, that **our brains do not differentiate between real pictures and vividly imagined ones!** We can scare ourselves easily with an imagined terrifying situation or story, and make our breathing and heart rate go up.

Remember, most of us mainly think with images or for those who are auditory learners, with an inner dialogue or monologue. Here is the catch that I have found from my observations of clients' communication: **Even though we think with images, about 95% of the time we are not consciously aware** that these pictures exist. The same is with our inner voice or sound. In the explanations and examples that I include below, I will focus on visual images, but remember that inner imagined voices and sounds have the same effect on our emotions and actions.

Our unawareness of these images does not hinder them from impacting us greatly. Our unconscious (which is another name for our old, or reptilian, brain) 'sees' these images and is directed by them. This means that visual images appear in our minds instantly when we use words, and our unconscious reacts immediately and forces our bodies to follow exactly, similar to when a bug flies towards you. You blink even before you process the information that it is a bug.

The act of saying something and initiating an image is like shining a flashlight around a dark room. The person you instruct, advise or give guidance sees only where you point the beam. This becomes the focus of our attention. (Thank you, Steve Andreas, for this beautiful metaphor!)

If used well, this beam (focus of our attention) illuminates what you really want or would like to ask a person to do. However, if not used well, it shines on something different or the opposite of what we want because we haven't chosen our words effectively (with the purpose of what we want them to see).

Where are you pointing your teen's attention?

Let me give you an example from a situation about which clients complain a lot – the morning rush. Stop for a second and think about the following scenario.

> "Wake up, we are going to be late again!" Pay attention to the image that you have brought to your child's mind. On what did you put your child's focus of attention? What does your child see? It's being late, isn't it?
>
> Now imagine that your child hears: "Wake up, we need to be on time!" What image have you created in his mind? Where is the focus of attention? Being on time, isn't it?
>
> "Late" and "on time" are two very different images and correspondently different focuses of attention. The words you use create different pictures/images. Where do you usually point that beam of light (focus of attention) for your teen? On being late? On being on time? Think about what you want them to do, and help your teens focus their attention on that image.

We have never been taught how the brain processes words, especially under time pressure or stress like the morning rush. In our example, in both statements parents want children to hurry up and be on time. By using, "…be late…" however, we create the opposite focus of attention/image of "being on time." Our intention is good, but our lack of knowledge about how our brains work causes us to make a huge mistake, which is miscommunication. Then we get frustrated when our children do not do what we told them to do.

Yet ironically, they are subconsciously following exactly and literally what you told them to do because you directed their attention to it through the image you created. It is like what address you put in their mind's Global Positioning System (GPS).

What address are you putting into your own mind's GPS?

Consider this: We do the same with ourselves in our inner monologues. How many times have you told yourself: *"I need to wake up, or I am going to be late*!" Sound familiar? Wrong GPS address! Wrong focus of attention! Our brains are literal when it comes to pictures in our mind! I hope you are going to remember this, would you? Isn't it better to say to yourself: *"I need to wake up to be on time*!"?

So, when you want a certain result or response, you need to stop for a moment and decide what kind of image (destination for the mind) you want to initiate in the person's mind, and only then formulate the instruction. In other words, on what do you want them to focus? Where do you want to send their attention?

To which image, voice, sound or feeling?

Instead of saying, "Get ready for your test or you will fail," you will get better results with saying, "Get prepared to pass your test." Another example is: "Stop stressing about that deadline." Change it to: "Relax and take your time. You can do this." And see what happens.

You'll notice that these examples of right and wrong communications are just statements. From what we've learned in Chapter 2 about the power of asking questions, we know there is a good chance that their impact will not be that high, and the brain could just ignore them by simply not hearing them (not processing).

Remember that asking a question instantly triggers the human brain to start to search relentlessly for an answer. We cannot NOT answer when there is a rise in tonality at the end of a sentence. The question grabs people's attention and sends their minds reeling to find an answer. But which answer? This is where focus comes into play. What images do your questions trigger? As with any powerful tool, we need to be careful to use questions in a way that helps people or at least avoids harming them. Using questions is like using a hammer - you can aim well and hit the nail on the head, or you can be careless and hurt yourself (or someone else).

In every field that I researched from marketing to

sciences, effective and influential communication approaches recommend using questions, and that **these questions should be good or right.**

What makes questions good or bad, right or wrong?

Most sources offer very long lists of the right questions to ask and the wrong ones to avoid. When I first started in coaching, I was learning from those long lists. Then I got lost and bored, finding it impossible to remember all the right questions, especially under time pressure in the situations when I needed them most. Moreover, even if there was a comprehensive list of right and wrong questions for all situations, it would be too complicated to remember and utilize.

This formula is different. It cracks the code of creating right (good) and wrong (bad) questions. It is exactly as I have explained above. **Everything depends on your wording and the resulting images (focus of attention) you create in the person's mind!**

With the correct wording, you can manage where your teens focus attention, therefore, guiding their behavior by stating something that provides a solution for their issue and is more helpful. You will not need to remember the list of right questions to ask or the wrong ones to avoid.

How does this part of the formula work?

Back to our earlier example of the morning hustle: "Wake up! You have to be on time!" This was a good shift that worked beautifully according to some parents I asked, but not according to all.

Now think how you can make your impact even more powerful (**instant, irresistible impact**) when you change the statement into a question: "Wake up! Do you want to be on time?" As you've learned, there is no way that a child's brain (ours too) could avoid creating an image of being 'on time' instantaneously! Then, when that image is there, you do not need to do anything. That image will guide all their decisions and actions in the direction you want: **to be on time**.

BEWARE of the opposite question, "Wake up, do you want to be late?" It has the same power to create an equal impact through the image of being late -- and make them late!

So, here we have two totally different pictures: One is the result of a *low-impact statement* and one is of a *high-impact question*. Let me ask you, which picture do you want your teens to have?

Here is a summary of the examples above.

	Low-Impact Statements	High-Impact Questions
Misleading destination	"Wake up! You are going to be **late**!"	"Wake up! Do you want to be **late**?"
Correct destination	"Wake up! You have to be **on time**!"	"Wake up! Do you want to be **on time**?"

I want to believe that you would choose, "Do you want to be **on time**?"

To get the result you want, decide what kind of image (destination for the mind) you would like to initiate in the person's mind, and then formulate your instruction as a question to have instant irresistible impact. For example, use "Are you ok?" instead of "What is wrong?" Use "Can you pay attention to what I say?" instead of "Can you stop ignoring me?" Even for very concrete situations, you can change the focus of attention. For instance, "Stop speeding up on curves!" can be altered to be more effective: "Can you please drive slowly here and be careful going around curves?"

When it is not easy to formulate a question, then simply add a 'tag question' after a statement at the end of the sentence. In this way, you will have that raised inflection of your voice to activate the brain and send it into a search. Here is an example from our previous situation: **"You want to be on time, don't you?"**

WANT YOUR TEEN TO LISTEN? •39

Figure 5 (A-D): Parent asks question with positive focus of attention versus positive statements

A)

B)

C)

D)

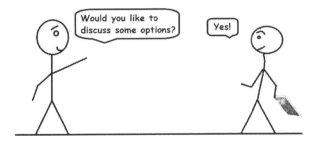

Over the past ten years, hundreds of parents have reported back to me that when they simply rephrased and initiated an image of being 'on time' instead of 'late' and posed it as a question, they saw a dramatic improvement in their teen's behavior. This simple shift of their teens' focus of attention on the right image helped them become 'on time' kids. For the entire family, this shift changed the whole morning flow, making the start of their days stress-free. Moreover, many parents also changed their inner monologues, because they also used to talk to themselves in terms of 'being late.' By choosing the right questions, they learned how to create the experience they wanted each day. There were positive results for everyone!

> ### A CLIENT'S SUCCESS STORY
>
> *As a child, I was raised with strict instructions and commands, which then pretty much became my parenting style. Building communication through natural engagement by asking the right questions was a big inner shift that opened up a completely different perspective. The skill works infallibly as soon as you know what question paints the picture you want your child to imagine.*
>
> *One day, my daughter called me screaming about a conflict with her college roommates. That day I decided to ask a question instead of my usual "stop stressing yourself out." The simple change in my language to "that is probably very uncomfortable. How do you see it resolved?" turned into a shortcut both in a conversation between us, and consequently the situation itself.*

Once you use this shortcut in your daily life, you'll look back and realize how long and how much energy it used to take to get your teen to listen, focus and cooperate! Even when things went smoothly, you may not have understood why or have been able to repeat what you said and achieve a similar outcome. You can see why I call this formula for asking resourceful questions a 'shortcut' – it's simple to use and the results are instant.

If you forget to formulate what you communicate as a question, here is a quick and smart trick to fix it: Simply complete your statement and add a tag question with rising intonation at the end.

Here is an example: "You want to remember to take your key with you, don't you?"

Remember my story of my daughter calling me in tears over once again forgetting her house key? Can you imagine how things changed in our household once I learned how to capture and guide her attention into a more resourceful direction?

There are ways that this might work with your teen, aren't there?

In a nutshell: To have irresistible instant impact and make your communication strong and effective, ask a question that has the "mind destination" you want the person to pursue, like putting the correct address into a GPS or pointing to an additional alternative.

This way of asking questions adds choice (it helps someone to get unstuck from focusing on only one thing) and provides flexibility (a person can choose) because it helps to focus and aim the person's attention and energy on a goal that is desired and beneficial or on one that should definitely be avoided.

45 • HOW TO GET YOUR TEEN TO LISTEN AND FOLLOW

Figure 6 (A-B): Parent gives helpful negative focus of attention

A)

B)

In other words, where do you want to send their attention, or on what do you want them to focus? Remember, as James Redfield said: "Where *Attention* goes Energy flows; Where *intention* goes Energy flows!"

I was excited to finally understand this concept and thought that my formula was complete when I remembered that there is one more important approach that can make it truly powerful. The use of negation!

CHAPTER 4

How to Keep Your Teen Listening with Negation

> *"Negation is much like reverse psychology. By telling the target not to do something, you slip a command into the sentence."*
>
> *– Christopher Hadnagy*

According to my observations, when asked what they want, 94-96% of people easily answer what they *do not* want, but it takes much more effort to formulate what they do want. How do we talk to our teens? Do we ask them to do what we want or do we direct them somewhere else?

Have you ever heard yourself saying, "Do not forget your keys!" Maybe when talking to your teen, you have even turned that command into a question: "Could you please not forget your keys?" Using the information from the previous chapters on questions and focus of attention, you now know that you have sent your teen's focus to something you do not want, haven't you?

"Do not forget..." is such a common phrase, heard often, especially when parents give instructions and advice. I questioned why "Do not forget" works so poorly, and then I discovered **that there is no picture for negatives like "no" or "not"**.

Everything fell into place. For me, this was another 'AHA' moment! I knew that negation influences our behavior and had used this tool for several years, but had not realized its deep impact until I learned that we think with images.

Let's explore how negation and negative words can dramatically either negate (ironic, isn't it?) your communication results or improve them. My inquiry was: "Can we use negation to create a negative or positive experience to direct a teen's attention, state, and behavior?"

My finding? We certainly can. There are two ways we can use it: to avoid traps of negation and in a smart way to add choices. Both approaches aim to increase the results of our communication by obtaining the responses we want.

What are the traps of negation?

The way we talk has become outdated because of the complete changes in our information environment that have occurred over the past 20 years. Our conversations usually have a lot of idioms, metaphors, sarcasm, humor, negation, and even double negation. Yet we hope that we are understood in the way we want to be comprehended.

Most of us, parents, teachers, and managers included, are **trapped in these miscommunication patterns, especially when giving instructions** or guidance. These patterns, however, are totally outdated for today's fast-paced environment. When we lack the time to process sophisticated language, our brains react to information literally. Sophisticated language has its place, but not when giving instructions or communicating for fast results under time pressure. I know that when you train animals, dogs especially, that you are taught to give succinct instructions for what you want the animal to do: sit, stay, heel, and then leave it at that. Would this work with people? Why don't we use negation with animals?

I heard this metaphor about how our brains process negation and appreciated its teaching power!

> If you hailed a taxi and instructed the taxi driver, "**DO NOT** take me to the airport," where do you think you would end up? Where would the driver take you? You

would expect the driver to take you anywhere else except the airport, right? However, you would most probably end up exactly where you did not want to go - to the airport.[15]

I was curious why our minds work this way. I would like to remind you that most of us **think with pictures/images and there are NO pictures for negation, negative words and some words with negative prefixes and suffixes.** These words exist in language, but not in how our brains make sense of the world.[16] Our brains need time to process the concept of negation, sometimes managing to grasp it, and often a bit late when the wrong action has already been taken.

---

[15] Daniel M. Wegner and David J. Schneider 'The White Bear Story', *Psychological Inquiry*, Volume 14, Number:3/4, p. 326–329, 2003: Daniel Wegner's Ironic Process Theory or white bear problem refers to the process, wherein deliberately trying to suppress certain thoughts makes them more likely to come to mind.

[16] Garner Thomson and Dr. Khalid Khan, *Magic in Practice: Introducing Medical NLP: the art and science of language in healing and health*, Hammersmith Books, Ltd., 2015.

52• HOW TO KEEP YOUR TEEN LISTENING WITH NEGATION

Figure 7 (A-C): Not smart use of negation

A)

B)

c)

How do we use negation?

- For negation we commonly use no, not, (do, be, have...) and the like with verbs and nouns.
- There are no images for negative words like neither, never, no one, nobody, none, nor, nothing, nowhere.
- We also use negative prefixes and suffixes sometimes. The most common negative prefixes are *de-*, *dis-*, *il-/ im-/ in-/ ir-*, *mis-*, *non-*, and *un-* (like **mis**understanding, **dis**qualified). The most common suffix is *–less* (like worth**less**, or use**less**).

Let's look at our earlier metaphor. If we imagine that our mind is a taxi driver who cannot process negation, then our instruction would be, "Take me to the airport."

Even if we make it into a question it would not bring any additional information to the mind's eye. In this case, the only word that makes sense and creates a picture in the taxi driver's mind is airport so that becomes our destination.

Remember, our mind/brain acts as a GPS and that GPS needs a picture as a destination, and it does not recognize negations for which pictures do not exist.

Think about when your teen was small, maybe you said, "Don't spill the milk!" What kind of image came to her mind? Correct, she would see an image of spilling the milk, and her mind would send those signals to her hands and most probably she would drop the cup. She would have already spilled it when the mind would just start to understand the negation. Our brain processes negation more slowly than it makes pictures in our mind, and usually after the body has already reacted accordingly.[17]

Now think about more critical situations. Imagine a scene in a movie or TV show in which a person is poised on the ledge of a building about to plunge to his death, and the negotiator says, "Don't jump." I cringe every time! The person on the ledge is at the peak of his emotion. In this situation, negotiators should be very

---

[17] Uri Hasson and Sam Glucksberg, 'Does understanding negation entail affirmation?: An examination of negated metaphors', *Journal of Pragmatics*, Volume 38, Issue 7, July 2006.

careful what they say because words create images which bring action.

Knowing what you now know about negation, don't you think that the only image the negotiator has created for the suicidal person with "Don't jump" is of jumping? In a matter of seconds, the suicidal person's literal brain has received its destination and is sending signals to his limbs to execute the action - and all this most probably before the rational mind could process the information to understand that it was, in fact, the opposite suggestion. Do you see from this example how there can be consequences to the way in which we use negation?

What other ways do you convey negation?

There are also some sneaky words that create the opposite of what you want. These include 'stop', 'quit,' 'avoid' or 'tired of.' Even though an instruction such as "Stop worrying!" contains no negation, it still states what you do not want them to do: 'worry' and that word is going to be the dominant one in the first image the brain creates. Think about that image: a person is in the process of stopping being worried. You don't see a calm person in that image, do you? Maybe instead of saying: "Quit your crying. It doesn't do any good," create a different destination – "Stay calm. How can I help?"

I suspect that many of us teach our teens to drive. Here are some examples from that activity.

- We don't **go** when the traffic light is red.

versus

We **stop** when the traffic light is red.

(This is a different 'stop', it shows an action itself and it has an image).

- Don't **speed up** there! You can get into an **accident**!

versus

Slow down here to be safe.

Our brain can process negation very effectively when there is enough processing time and conscious attention applied. Interestingly though, I have found from observations and practice that repeating the same negation in situations that are not stressful has the same effect on our minds as when it is used under time pressure and stress. For example, if I repeatedly tell my daughter, "do not forget to take out the trash," and it is not a stressful situation, then she will still forget.

> *A CLIENT'S STORY*
>
> *When I was participating in Viktoria's workshop I had to laugh out loud. I had given my son a house key for the first time and was very serious about making sure that he takes care of it. Very persuasively and with a strong voice, I looked into his eyes and said, "Promise not to lose it! Promise?" When hearing my story, the whole workshop group burst into laughter, when I said, "It worked! He lost it on the same day!"*

How do we use negation in a smart way?

Pay attention to what you say when asked what you want. Remember, for most people, it is much easier to say what they do not want than what they want. Pain is a more powerful motivator than pleasure. With this knowledge, however, using carefully crafted negation can become your best tool in influencing your teens and other people, and getting the results you want in your communication.

When it comes to negation there are two approaches.

#1 The first one is simple: you give the correct action without any negation.

Remember our negotiator with the suicidal person on the ledge, telling him, "Don't jump?"

When your teens are in an emotional state, it's the same as if they are poised on the ledge of the building! Instead, tell them what you want them to do, not what you don't want. Instead of "Don't jump!" you will be more effective saying, "**Stay there!**" or "**Hold on.**" Instead of "Do not shoot!" it is better to say, "**Put the gun down!**" Instead of "Don't be nervous," or "Stop being nervous!" it is better to use "**Stay calm.**" You have given the brain two very different destinations. Compare "You shouldn't take off your sweater, it is cold." with "**Keep your sweater on**, it is cold."

WANT YOUR TEEN TO LISTEN? • 59

Figure 8 (A-C): Smart use of negation

A)

B)

#2 This approach helps you express the same message (almost the same), but in a way that helps your unconscious know what you would prefer instead. For example, you could say, "I'm **not comfortable**" instead of "I **am stressed**." Since there is no image for 'not' your literal unconscious mind sees an image of you being comfortable and can initiate the process of taking you exactly where you want to be – comfortable.

Another example is when your teen says, "This is too difficult to do!" You can use the same 'sleight of mouth' and change it into (as well as acknowledge her feeling): "I agree, it is **not** easy to do!" You have the same meaning to convey, but you have created a totally different image and therefore an impact on her mind.

Figure 9 (A-B): Sophisticated use of negation

Remember, our brain is pretty literal and mechanical under stress. Tell the brain what you want and it'll help you achieve it. This shift of attention has a tremendous impact on people, and especially on our children. This is why humans are extremely easily manipulated, because our bodies react before our brains process.

In a nutshell: Skillful use of negation has tremendous and instant impact in getting the outcome you want. When it is formulated as a question with a clear focus of attention then it becomes irresistible.

CHAPTER 5

How to Get Irresistible Instant Cooperation with Your Teen

> *"Quality questions create a quality life. Successful people ask better questions, and as a result, they get better answers."*
>
> *– Tony Robbins*

Let's now combine the information we've learned from the previous three chapters to finalize the 3 pieces of the formula:

- ⇒ Use questions to more powerfully catch and hold attention
- ⇒ Guide focus of attention on images, voices, and feelings which act as a GPS destination for the mind
- ⇒ Employ the smart use of negation

These three actions form an extremely effective tool that will enable you to have influence on anyone anytime. Instead of feeling exasperated with your teen and maybe even with yourself, you will say, "Oh! In this situation, I know exactly which question to ask to get the response I want!"

Figure 10 (A-D): The Attention Guiding Questions[SM] (AGQ) Formula

A)

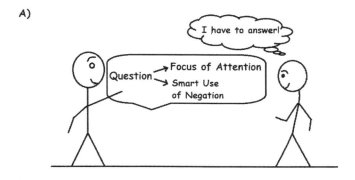

B)

C)

D)

For some time during my research, I had been calling this 3-action formula 'goal-positioning' questions. I also was caught in positivity. I thought, "Goals should be affirmative!" This means you should carefully use words in a way that you talk about what you want people to do, or think about, instead of what you do *not* want them to do. Remember, we often need to bring a teen's attention to the negative consequences of their intentions or behaviors. If your teen wants to go to a party without knowing anybody there, would you want to bring her attention to a possible danger of not having anybody watching her back? In this case, the question should bring her attention to the uncomfortable or dangerous images.

People I had taught were amazed at how powerful asking these kinds of questions can be. The second wave of 'WOW' reactions came from parents who reported back how effective the method was after using the shortcut with their children. I then thought to call them 'empowering questions' but this felt too general and did not give any idea of what the question does. So, I decided to name this formula by exactly what the questions do: **Attention Guiding Questions**^{SM} or **AGQs**^{SM}.

Remember, our questions function as triggers for the brain to find an answer. As I shared previously - when we create the correct image with our questions, we do the following:

- add choice – this helps someone to get unstuck so they are not over-focusing on only one thing

- provide flexibility so a person can choose.

This helps teens to focus and direct attention and energy on a goal that they really want and can benefit from,

or

the converse: from taking actions they should definitely avoid.

AGQs make your communication even more powerful because your questions can catch and again redirect your teen's attention on something that is either a solution and/or more helpful.

The following example will demonstrate what I mean. You hear: "Mom, I am going to fail my test!" This means that your teen has a picture of himself right in front of his mind's eye. In this picture he is failing. So to change this picture, you ask, "Do you want to pass your test?" Your seemingly simple question does several things:

1. Your teen cannot help but to create an image in his mind because you triggered his brain to go and find an answer.
2. That image is of him passing his test. Now he has two images in front of him, one that may be to his advantage.
3. Because there are two images, he now has options.

You added choices and new possibilities. This flexibility to choose empowers your teen!

Keep in mind that when you do not know the power of asking questions, you might accidentally and very often limit a person or even cause harm. We can use our previous example, "Wake up, do you want to be late?" or another one, "Do you want to hurt yourself?" or "Why are you so stupid?" Are these good pictures to create in a person's mind? Do they empower the person?

Of course, the same principle works for asking ourselves questions. Think about what kind of image some people create as a GPS destination for their minds when they ask themselves, often repetitively, "Why am I so stupid?" or "Why did I do that?" These kinds of questions and the concurrent images you create with them are not going to help!

There are better questions to ask to create better destinations for our unconscious mind. For example, "What can I do to act better next time?" instead of, "Why I am so stupid?" Instead of, or after, "Why did I do that?" I would suggest asking yourself, "What steps can I take next time to do that differently?" or something similar that will create resourceful images.

Remember that in creating the AGQs, you can use negation to your (or your teen's) advantage in the smart way I explained in Chapter 4. The example below shows a more elaborated version of the above example.

> "Mom, I am so **nervous**! I'm **afraid** I'll **fail** my test."

Here are three different possible responses this daughter can get from Mom:

> #1 A parent would usually say, "**Stop** being **nervous** and **afraid**! You are not going to fail!"

Is that helpful? What images have been created for this teen? The same that she had with her own statements – being nervous and afraid! Nothing is added or changed with that good intention. The teen will continue to have the feelings she asked for help to change.

> #2 Let's try another positive common approach. "What can we do to help you *stop* being **nervous** and **afraid** and be able *not* to **fail**?"

Would this help? According to what we have learned about questions sending our minds to find answers, and how negatives and sneaky words (like 'stop') function, then this question can make the images even more intense. These are not destinations that we want a teen's mind to pursue!

> #3 What if we use the powerful instant-impact communication that AGQs provide? This question would instantly change the focus of attention by creating images that are more resourceful, providing a different destination for the mind to pursue: "I understand that you are *not* **confident** about **passing** your test. Would you like to **calm** down and be **more focused** to be able to **pass** your test?"

As you can see, with careful wording we can create those pictures in the teen's mind that are a better destination: calm, focused, and passing the test.

More examples are given below.

FLASHLIGHT IN A DARK ROOM – TRAPS TO AVOID

Trap #1 - Word Choice

Creating the WRONG IMAGE	Creating the RIGHT IMAGE
We will **be late**! Do you want to be **late**?	You have to be **on time**! Do you want to **be on time**?
Don't **forget** to take your key. You are not going to **forget** the key, are you?	**Remember** to take the key. Can you **remember** to take the key?
You will **fail** your test if you go to that party. Do you want to **fail** your test because of that party?	To **pass** your test you need that time to study. Do you want to **pass** your test and this time skip that party?

What do you emphasize? Being late or being on time? Forgetting or remembering? Failing or passing? Remember to check where you have focused the person's attention.

Trap #2 - Negation

A) NO and NOT

Creating the WRONG IMAGE	Creating the RIGHT IMAGE
Do not **open** that box!	Leave the **box closed**!
Can you please not **open** that box?	Can you **leave the box closed**, please?

To make sense of what not to do, your brain first creates an image of opening the box, doesn't it?

Creating the WRONG IMAGE	Creating the RIGHT IMAGE
No **drinking is** allowed in the teen club!	Stay **sober**!
Do you promise not **to drink**?	Do you promise to **stay sober**?

What image does this initiate in a teen's mind? GRATEFULLY THERE IS AN OPPOSITE FOR DRUNK - "SOBER". Smoking does not have an opposite – we use only smoke-free, which does not help in this case.

B) NEITHER and NEVER

Creating the WRONG IMAGE	Creating the RIGHT IMAGE
Never **lie** again!	**Telling the truth** would help you more.
You will never **lie** again, will you?	Can you **tell the truth**?

The mind sees an image of doing it again and then tries to see an image of not doing, which turns out to be impossible to see and the person ends up doing the activity again. The solution here, especially while instructing children is to give an option of what to do.

C) NO ONE, NOBODY, NOWHERE, NONE, NOTHING

Creating the WRONG IMAGE	Creating the RIGHT IMAGE
Do not **worry, nobody** is in the room!	**Stay calm,** the room is empty.
Can you trust me that **nobody** is in the room?	**Stay calm** - would you like me to check the room?

Imagine the image the brain receives... Worry, someone is in the room!

Trap #3 - Sneaky Words

A) <u>STOP</u>

<u>Creating the WRONG IMAGE</u>	<u>Creating the RIGHT IMAGE</u>
Stop **worrying**.	Stay **calm**.
Will you stop **worrying**?	How can I help you **stay calm**?

The first image created is that of a worrying person.

B) <u>QUIT</u>

<u>Creating the WRONG IMAGE</u>	<u>Creating the RIGHT IMAGE</u>
Quit **talking back to me**.	Please **speak** to me with respect.
Will you quit **talking back**?	Could you **speak respectfully,** please?

The person will continue doing the action if you give them the wrong image.

I have presented both low- and high-impact sentences

(statements vs. questions), which create a mind image we want the listener to pursue.

On the physical level, the AGQ formula creates an exact/literal image in the brain of what we want the person to pursue or avoid. Remember, when you ask the AGQs you direct a people's attention to something from which they can benefit or not. When you knowingly ask AGQs you can tremendously help because in doing so, you add new perspectives and choices to that person's limiting focus of attention.

A CLIENT'S SUCCESS STORY

I either used commands or open-ended questions with my 17-year-old son who constantly showed resistance. He was left with no choice to make his own decisions, but could only follow up with what I had already decided for him. I am sure many parents are familiar with such resistance. For example, I was saying "You have the SAT test this year, so you have to check your calendar and set up time to ensure you practice and prepare enough". Guess what the answer was: "I will think about it".

However, after having read the book I have changed my commands into questions that are formulated in a way to focus his attention and provide him with choices to decide but at the same time get him to cooperate. Using "Attention Guiding Questions", my talk to my teen about SATs, became: "Do you want to get a high score on the SAT?" And then, after some pause, "What do you think needs to be done?" The question drew his immediate attention to the key pictures of "high score" and "what to do to have a high score". AGQs really are powerful.

Benefits of using the AGQ formula in your communication

You perhaps can see how asking a question is one of the most influential tools in human communication. I would add to this idea that the most influential tool in human communication is storytelling. The most effective storytelling uses a lot of smoothly embedded questions that capture, maintain and guide the listener's attention. Questions help the listeners experience the story as if it were happening to them. You engage people and your story will have them hanging onto the edge of their seats to find out where it is going. If you use AGQs in your storytelling, then your guidance becomes irresistible.

"What's right in your life?" vs. "What's wrong with your life?"

As we bring back the metaphor of a flashlight beam in the dark room, the following happens when you use the AGQ formula: You move the beam from what is wrong in life to what is right. Or, if you want to warn that something can go wrong, you move the beam and point to those wrong things. In both cases, we add new perspectives.

For example: **"What would happen if you miss that class? Would it cause you to fail your test?"**

The beauty of asking AGQs is that images are

automatically created in your teen's mind, which means you reach your parental goal of having your teen listen and process what you are saying. However, this is done in a very gentle way because you guide, not command, which would cause resistance and dampen rapport. Offered gently, you are empowering and teaching your teens to make their own choices.

All teens, despite their behavior and what they say, want to be loved, appreciated and respected. This approach of using the AGQ formula might become one of the best manifestations of your love and care in an inventively gentle way. With this skill, you can begin to more effectively reinforce all your guidance in preparing your teen for an independent life.

With AGQs I found my formula or shortcut to improve my communication with my teen! And now you can use this formula too!

In the Conclusion, you will learn how to remember to use the AGQ formula every time you talk to your teen.

CONCLUSION

How to Recall the AGQ^{SM} Formula Every Time You Speak

> *"Knowing others is intelligence;
> knowing yourself is true wisdom.
> Mastering others is strength;
> mastering yourself is true power."*
>
> *– Lao Tzu*

My experience in working with clients, and as a mother, have enabled me to get the gist of parental complaints these days. The main problematic areas include the following: Our kids don't listen and parenting leaves us feeling guilty and incompetent when our teens bring out the worst in us. So, instead of giving you a long list of Dos and Don'ts, I have given you this short book with effective ways to end your struggle with your teen by using **my simple formula, Attention Guiding Questions (AGQs), based on behavioral science and the art of cooperation.**

I want to make sure you also know that this is just the **first of 3 formulas** I've developed to help you and your relationship with your teen even more: the second is conflict prevention, and the third is about staying calm and resourceful in difficult times. I'll tell you more about that a little later.

Summing it all up

Before you open your mouth to talk to your teen, stop for a moment and turn anything you want to say into questions, even better, into Attention Guiding Questions. That's it! This is the formula! Let me repeat that it is *irresistible in its instant impact*. Your teen might know that you use AGQs, but they cannot resist anyway, for two reasons:

1. Answering questions and following your lead for focus of attention is innate and nobody cannot NOT follow it. (How long did it take you to process this double negation?)
2. Asking questions demonstrates respect, and therefore bypasses resistance.

We have discussed the direct benefits of asking the AGQ: capturing and holding your teen's attention; helping them see the consequences of their actions, choices or taking no action; and redirecting their attention to something that is resourceful - because when you ask AGQs your teen will not be able to help but physically hear and process your concerns, instructions, guidance and advice.

Allow me to expand on this. Asking teens (or anyone) AGQs benefits both parents and teens because you:

- Demonstrate that you are willing to put effort into understanding them
- Show that you value and accept their opinion and boost their self-esteem
- Learn more about them and what is going on with them (their present circumstances)
- Give them opportunities to find solutions and make decisions (you do not take away their potential!)
- Show you are respectful of their efforts to become independent and find their identity
- Teach them to be responsible and accountable for their decisions
- Enable your teen to model and learn from your behavior

As soon as you use the AGQ formula, you will see how extraordinary the results can be. **Our teens just want to be loved, appreciated, respected, and, yes, guided and guarded even though they may not even realize it. Knowing how to use these questions may become one of the best expressions of your love and care during these important years.** As I said in the very beginning of this book, once you master this formula, you will be confident in helping your teen face any situation, and in bringing peacefulness into your home for now and into the future.

Can you now picture this happening in your family?

Using AGQs helped me to get my daughter back. She is no longer the non-communicative stranger living under my roof. Now she smiles at us and interacts with us instead of having her head hanging over her phone all the time!

For some of you, just reading this book and learning about Attention Guiding Questions might be enough for you to take it in and make it your everyday tool. You may use the knowledge from this book right away and it will work beautifully. You will remember to ask AGQs every time you need to guide, protect and help your teen.

However, for many of us, this is not the case. Remember, there is a difference between intellectual knowledge and skills. Knowledge can be learned, but most of us need to put in effort to remember to use it. When we remember to use our knowledge automatically, it becomes a skill that can run on autopilot or feel like second-nature.

There is also a limit when learning from written text for two major reasons:

1. According to Albert Mehrabian, 93% of our emotional communication is nonverbal. It is known as "the 7%-38%-55% Rule" where 55% of a message we convey comes through body language, 38% the tone of voice and audio/sounds we make, and 7% through the actual words spoken.[18] A written text can be misinterpreted easily. In the current teen text-messaging world, a lot of dramas are happening! How effective is it to learn from a written text? We know that most of us learn, remember and automate knowledge better from a teacher and in a classroom from peers!

2. We learn new behavior and make it automatic in three ways:

- **Instant or one-trial learning**: After only one experience the knowledge becomes your automatic behavior. I believe some of you are these kinds of learners. An easy example is: after touching a hot stove you would never do it again! It is like a phobia, wherein we usually need one experience to make it our automatic reaction. In most cases, it must be extremely emotionally charged to remember and to make that conditioned response run automatically. Pavlov's dog might have learned a response with one trial if it was painful. Instead, it learned to create an association between getting fed and

---

[18] Albert Mehrabian, (http://www.iojt-dc2013.org/~/media/Microsites/Files/IOJT/11042013-Albert-Mehrabian-Communication-Studies.ashx)

the sound of the bell after several repetitions. For a no-pain or emotion-involved (for humans) experience, live creatures need repetition to create an association.

- **Many repetitions**: There is an old Latin saying engraved in stone, "Repetition is the mother of all learning." According to different studies, you need from 21 to 90 days on average to build new simple automatic habits. I am not talking about a habit that involves addiction. For example, give children a piece of candy only twice and you can easily develop a habit of them wanting candy every time they are in the same situation. We are talking about helpful habits like drinking more water, exercising, studying, asking questions instead of making statements, focusing on positives instead of negatives, paying attention to one's own thoughts and so on. Not all of them are pleasant at the beginning, but we can make them run automatically after several repetitions.

- **Special techniques**: We usually think that learning new behavior is pretty hard, but it is not. There are techniques that accelerate this process and make it automatic. Remember, 95% of our behaviors are conditioned responses. There are ways to make new habits form much faster using the patterns of conditioned responses, visualization and a very special set of techniques developed by different behavior modification fields.

Wondering how you will ever remember how to use AGQs?

Well, based on the research on learning behavior that I just described, here is a set of exercises that will help you get started in embedding this information – and any information, anytime.

This technique uses Visual, Auditory and Kinesthetic (feeling or physical sensation) reminders to be used for at least 90 days. I use this, among other, techniques with my clients and during workshops as a first step in breaking unhelpful habits and developing new resourceful habits. If you would like to learn more about other techniques, visit my website

www.Live-in-Harmony.com

as this is the only one that can be taught in written form.

The 3-senses reminder process

The process I'm going to share helps you practice saying all your statements or commands in the form of a question. It is a commitment over time, but it is very effective at accelerating your learning a new habit. You will love the results for you, for your relationship with your teen, and others who will benefit from your new communication skills!

VISUAL REMINDER. You need a red pen and at least 20, preferably yellow, stickers such as a Post-it®.

Write the following words on each sticker: I want to ask [your teen's name] questions. Then post it all over your living, sleeping and working space, on places that your eyes will see many times during a day to act as a frequent reminder: a bathroom mirror, on the fridge, your calendar, wallet, car dashboard, computer and phone screen, and so on. If it is appropriate, the best places are on photographs of your teen and your teen's room door.

When you're tempted to make a statement, such as, "Clean your room, please!" you will now be reminded that you are to make it an AGQ, "When are you going to clean your room?"

Random places will help to train your mind and remember to use questions instead of commands. Your teen's room door will help you the most. The sticker on the photograph will create an association in your mind: Whenever you see your teen and want to say something, anything, turn it into a question. That will also help you to understand what is going on with them, listen to what they say and then offer whatever you want to offer.

Special note: Using red plays a special role in catching your conscious and unconscious attention. The reason for using yellow for the stickers is that it provides high contrast with the red, and serves as an instant and consistent reminder every time you see it.

KINESTHETIC REMINDER. I strongly suggest wearing a new ring or band/bracelet on your wrist for at least 90 days as a tactile/kinesthetic reminder (you can change it to a new one once in a while when you feel you've gotten used to it). It will trigger a reminder that you want to ask a question in the AGQ formula instead of making a statement or giving an order! It should not feel too comfortable, so that you will notice it, and it will remind you. These kinds of triggers are meant to help you to change your default pattern to a more useful habit.

AUDITORY REMINDER. For the auditory reminder, you need to make an association between asking questions and your teen's name. That is why I suggest you put your teen's name on the stickers. After several days whenever you say your teen's name or somebody else says the name, you will associate it with asking questions. So, the Visual Reminder helps to create the Auditory Reminder.

Here is what this 3-senses reminder process does: It **ADJUSTS YOUR MIND GPS** on what you want to do, which is to ask questions anytime you want to talk to your teen. When you commit to this practice, it will become your new behavior. Don't be surprised when you notice that you are using the AGQ formula with other people too.

Would you like to be supported and guided?

While referring to the text, practicing AGQs on your own, and using the 3-senses reminder process will certainly help you, more personal and practical support can be invaluable for you to truly understand and embed this powerful formula, and to know how to apply it to your individual teen(s) and situation, with guidance along the way.

In my individual and group coaching I focus on helping parents with the following:

- Exploring AGQs more deeply, and working on accelerated techniques to make asking AGQs a skill and shortcut that becomes second-nature. You will be able to call upon these skills in any situation, especially when there is stress or time pressure involved. I wish I could teach the same skills simply through written text but it does not work that way! There is nothing like the personal contact, and what we also learn from each other in groups.

And remember the other 2 formulas I mentioned earlier? These are other crucial areas that need to be addressed: conflict prevention and staying calm and resourceful. I have developed simple formulas for these important skills as well, and I am teaching these in my coaching with great results. Also, two books are in the works, to be published soon, on each of these topics.

Are Your Parenting Skills Up to Date?

Check www.Live-in-Harmony.com/Parenting-Teens for a free assessment to help you find out.

For more information on my one-on-one, group, and VIP coaching and parenting introductory workshops that can help you to make using Attention Guiding Questions and other skills your default mode, visit

www.Live-in-Harmony.com/parenting-teens

Here you will also find additional helpful resources on my **Shift Teen Behavior System**.

I would like to hear your comments and stories. I'd love to answer any questions you have. Please feel free to email me:

tervika@live-in-harmony.com

Here is to your success in reconnecting with your teens and being laser persuasive with anyone.

Viktoria Ter-Nikoghosyan

San Francisco 2017

About the Author

Acclaimed International Personal and Professional Development Consultant and Coach, Viktoria Ter-Nikoghosyan, Ph.D., has helped hundreds of parents in 23 countries to reconnect with their teens to guard and guide them effectively through the adolescent years and into independent life. She has learned from many of the best in their fields. She is the mother of three happy and successful children: two adults and one teen.

Dr. Ter-Nikoghosyan credits her success with clients to the fact that, because of her background, she understands how to naturally change your biochemistry to influence your emotions, behavior, performance, and health.

Before becoming involved in personal development, she had several successful and lucrative careers that have led her from a Ph.D. in Biophysics to being an international consultant on organizational development, and serving as a consultant to the United Nations. In addition to 13 years of pure academic experience, she also has 18 years of combined research, leadership, advising and training experience in different fields including environment, law, economics, human development, and the ICT industry.

Viktoria has provided her services in three languages (English, Russian and Armenian) to diverse organizations and individuals, such as United Nations officials, company executives, business teams, high-ranking public officials, lead opera singers, musicians, athletes, and scientists in several countries. They all have made dramatic changes to their lives.

She also does pro bono work at women's shelters training psychologists how to help victims (including teens) of abuse and domestic violence. This entails teaching them to overcome PTS and learn Emotional Intelligence skills to protect themselves and move on in their lives.

Viktoria provides additional support to parents through group, one-on-one, and VIP programs, which help parents reconnect with their teens and bring peace back into their families.

www.Live-in-Harmony.com/parenting-teens

Visit
www.Live-in-Harmony.com/Parenting-Teens

TO BE THE FIRST TO KNOW
about upcoming books
by Dr. Viktoria Ter-Nikoghosyan

DOES YOUR TEEN PUSH YOUR BUTTONS?
The Proven Formula to Keep Calm and Have Self-Control while Dealing with Teenagers

WANT YOUR TEEN TO STOP FIGHTING WITH YOU?
The Proven Irresistible Formula to Convince Teens To Avoid Mistakes and Make Sound Decisions

---

HOW ARE YOU DOING AS A PARENT?
Take a free self-assessment to help you find out at
www.Live-in-Harmony.com/parenting-teens

You also can connect with me to learn about the supportive community that is actively engaged and excited about using these formulas.

Made in the USA
Middletown, DE
03 December 2018